Grant Seeking Basics

A No-Frills, No-Nonsense Guidebook for Beginners

Grant Seeking Basics
A No-Frills, No-Nonsense Guidebook for Beginners

Merlene Alicia Vassall, JD

Mount Rainier, MD

Grant Seeking Basics
A No-Frills, No-Nonsense Guidebook for Beginners
by Merlene Alicia Vassall, JD

Technical Assistance & Support Consultants
P.O. Box 69
Mount Rainier, MD 20712-2111 U.S.A.
http://www.technicalassistance.com

ISBN-13: 978-0-983-40880-2

Cover art by Kevin Richardson, Kebo Designs

Printed in the United States of America

INTRODUCTION

Philanthropy is a huge "industry." According to the Foundation Center's *Foundation Growth and Giving Estimates, 2010 Edition*, there were 75,000 grantmaking foundations in the United States in 2009. These foundations awarded $42.9 billion in grant support, despite the economic crisis.

Yet, the funds provided by foundations pale in comparison to the dollars distributed by the Federal Government. Grants.gov -- the central storehouse for information -- provides access to approximately $500 billion annually through more than 1,000 grant programs that provide funding and assistance to state and local governments, public and private profit and nonprofit organizations, specialized groups, and individuals.

Clearly, grant money is available for nonprofit organizations that are able to:

- sort through the many grantmaking programs,

- prepare high-quality proposals, and

- maintain good relationships with funders.

Designed for new development personnel as well as more experienced staff members who seek to refresh and refine their skills, this document provides a step-by-step guide to:

- get yourself and your organization ready for fundraising;

- identify funding prospects;

- develop a fundraising plan and make your plan work;

- prepare credible and compelling proposals;

- build long-term relationships with funders; and

- evaluate your efforts.

This guidebook also identifies resources -- publications, websites, and organizations -- that can help streamline and simplify the grantseeking process.

I. GET READY FOR FUNDRAISING

The first step in any fundraising campaign is to "get your house in order." This is especially true for new organizations. The following are the major steps you should take to ensure that you and your organization are ready to begin approaching grantmakers:

A. **Take care of prerequisite administrative/management matters.**

1. Incorporate. Visit the website of your state's corporations division for forms and instructions.

2. Obtain 501(c)(3) federal tax-exempt status. To obtain Package 1023 - Application for Recognition of Exemption, contact:

   Internal Revenue Service
   http://www.irs.ustreas.gov/charities/charitable/index.html

3. Obtain local tax-exempt status. Visit the websites of your state's and locality's taxation divisions for forms and instructions.

4. Register to solicit funds. To request information on requirements, forms, and fee schedules, contact each state in which you plan to conduct fundraising activities. (You can find their contact information at http://www.multistatefiling.org/.) If you plan to register in multiple states, obtain the Unified Registration Statement from:

   Multi-State Filer Project
   http://www.multistatefiling.org/

5. Adhere to generally accepted accounting procedures (i.e., get a qualified accountant to manage your finances).

6. Comply with standards for charities. To request a copy of standards promulgated by the major "watchdog" group, contact:

   BBB Wise Giving Alliance
   www.give.org

B. Develop a mission statement.

This standard, internally agreed-upon statement describes your organization's purpose, general methods, and target population. For example:

1. "The Foundation Center is an independent nonprofit organization established by foundations in 1956. Our mission is to increase public understanding of the foundation field. We do this by maintaining a comprehensive and up-to-date database on foundations and corporate giving programs, by producing directories, and by analyzing trends in foundation support of the nonprofit sector."

2. "Technical Assistance & Support Consultants (TASC) assists progressive organizations in meeting their development needs. To help organizations promote themselves among their potential constituency bases and prospective funders, TASC offers a range of services in the areas of fund development, writing and publishing, and grantsmanship training."

3. "The Council of Better Business Bureaus, a nonprofit membership organization of ethical businesses, promotes truth and fairness in the marketplace and protects consumers through voluntary self-regulation and monitoring activities."

C. Develop an annual program plan. (See sample.) For each of your organization's programs, define the following:

1. goal -- the overall outcome you seek to realize

2. objectives -- the specific, measurable results you seek to achieve to realize your overall goal

3. target population(s)

4. program site(s)

5. collaborations with other organizations

6. personnel

7. milestones -- target dates for major activities

ANNUAL PROGRAM PLAN

(Note: An organization with several programs would complete several forms.)

PROGRAM NAME: Foster Care Research Project

Program Goal: To prompt policy and practice changes to benefit local children and families in the foster care system by developing and disseminating a research report

Objectives:
a. To compile comprehensive data not currently accessible to the public
b. To prepare a useful, reader-friendly research report with policy and practice recommendations
c. To generate media coverage and public attention to the plight of children in foster care

Target Populations:
a. Local policymakers
b. Local program administrators
c. Local advocacy groups
d. Local media

Program Sites:
a. My City, USA

Collaborating Organizations:
a. Association of Concerned Social Workers
b. Children's Advocacy Network
c. Local College, School of Social Work

Primary Personnel (Percentage of their Time Spent on this Project):
a. Executive Director (10%)
b. Deputy Director for Children's Programs (50%)
c. Deputy Director for Research (50%)
d. Research Associate (50%)
e. Secretary (25%)

Milestones:
a. Finalize research plan - January 15
b. Complete data collection - June 15
c. Complete first draft of report - August 30
d. Complete second draft of report - September 30
e. Complete committee review process - October 15
f. Finalize and print report - November 15
g. Release report at press conference - December 15
h. Disseminate report through mass mailing and Internet - December 20

Technical Assistance & Support Consultants

D. **Develop an organizational chart.** (See sample.) This chart provides a visual representation of your organizational structure.

E. **Develop project budgets and an annual budget for the entire organization.** (See sample project budget.)

1. List projected expenses.

   a. Salaries

   b. Program Expenses

   c. Administrative (Overhead or Office) Expenses

2. List projected income, indicating whether each line item has been received or is anticipated.

3. Make sure all dollar amounts are real and reasonable figures. Get price quotes from vendors, and find out salaries of individuals in comparable positions.

4. Include budget notes where appropriate to explain how you arrived at your figures and/or what materials or services each figure encompasses.

5. Always include at least a portion of overhead expenses and administrative personnel in project budgets.

6. Administrative (overhead) and fundraising expenses combined should comprise no more than 35% of the total expenses.

SAMPLE ORGANIZATIONAL CHART

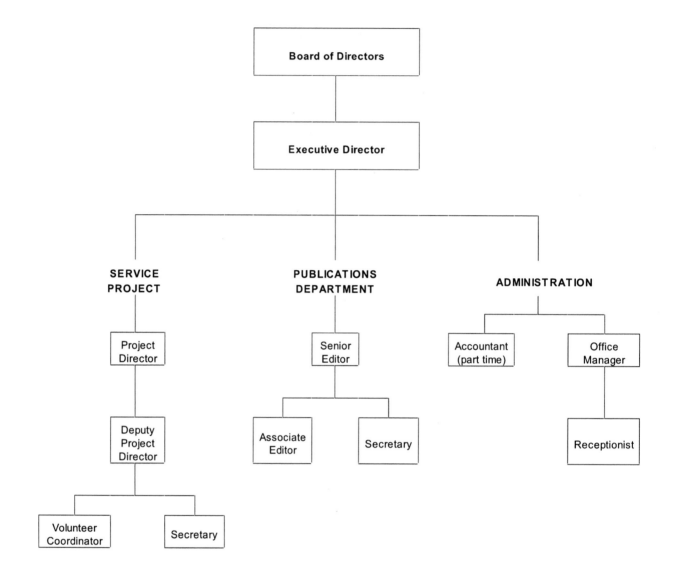

SAMPLE PROJECT BUDGET

Salaries & Benefits		Year One		Year Two[1]
Executive Director (20% of $120,000)	$	24,000	$	25,200
Program Director (100% of $90,000)	$	90,000	$	94,500
Deputy Program Director (100% of $70,000)	$	70,000	$	73,500
Volunteer Coordinator (100% of $64,000)	$	64,000	$	67,200
Accountant (10% of $70,000)	$	7,000	$	7,350
Administrative Assistant (50% of $48,000)	$	24,000	$	25,200
Benefits (20% of salaries)	$	55,800	$	58,590
Subtotals	**$**	**334,800**	**$**	**351,540**
Program Expenses				
Advisory Committee Honorariums[2]	$	7,500	$	0
Printing of Manual[3]	$	750	$	788
Production of Public Service Announcement	$	2,000	$	0
Six Counseling Sessions[4]	$	3,000	$	3,150
Miscellaneous	$	500	$	525
Subtotal	**$**	**13,750**	**$**	**4,463**
Administrative Expenses				
Rental of Office & Utilities	$	12,000	$	12,600
Telephones	$	2,400	$	2,520
Delivery/Postage	$	1,800	$	1,890
Supplies	$	3,600	$	3,780
Photocopying	$	1,200	$	1,260
Subtotal	**$**	**21,000**	**$**	**22,050**
TOTAL EXPENSES	**$**	**369,550**	**$**	**378,053**
Secured Income				
Carnegie Corporation of New York	$	150,000	$	150,000
Ford Foundation	$	100,000	$	100,000
Cafritz Foundation	$	50,000	$	0
Subtotal	**$**	**300,000**	**$**	**250,000**
Anticipated Income				
Meyer Foundation	$	25,000	$	0
Rockefeller Foundation	$	25,000	$	0
Combined Federal Campaign	$	10,000	$	10,000
Program Registration Fees	$	10,000	$	10,000
Subtotal	**$**	**70,000**	**$**	**20,000**
TOTAL INCOME	**$**	**370,000**	**$**	**270,000**

[1]A five percent increase to cover inflation has been calculated for expense items in Year Two
[2]Ten members, three meetings, $250 honorarium per meeting per member
[3]500 copies printed @ $1.50 each
[4]Space rental @ $200 per session, refreshments @ $300 per session

F. Decide what types of support you need:

1. general support funds -- unrestricted funds

2. special project funds -- to support a specific program

3. planning grant funds -- to support the planning of a new program

4. seed money -- to help begin a new program or organization

5. capital campaign funds -- for a building or endowment

6. program related investments -- a loan

7. emergency funds

8. in-kind donations -- equipment, supplies, or services

G. Gather needed information and extra copies of "supplies" to keep on hand:

1. existing proposals, solicitation letters, reports, and organizational literature

2. Federal Identification Number

3. DUNS Number (www.dnb.com)

4. IRS 501(c)(3) letter

5. bylaws

6. articles of incorporation

7. list of board of directors

8. list of advisory committee members (if applicable)

9. job descriptions

10. résumés

11. organizational chart

12. annual report

13. IRS 990 Form

14. financial statements/audit

15. organizational budgets (last year, this year, and next year)

16. newspaper clippings

17. brochures and publications

18. letters of support by clients, experts, and/or community leaders

II. DEVELOP A FUNDRAISING PLAN

Although some fundraisers can function without a written plan, the planning process will make your efforts more effective. Planning forces you to think ahead, organize and prioritize your ideas, and consider various "what if" situations. It also enables you to respond intelligently to grantmakers who want to know what your fundraising plans are. Here is a process for developing a fundraising plan for your organization:

A. Develop annual fundraising goals. (See sample.)

1. Establish an overall goal for total funds to be raised for the year. This should be based on your organization's expense budget.

2. To meet your overall goal, establish target amounts to be raised from various sources of income. Use last year's actual figures or speak to organizations that have conducted similar fundraising activities to help you make realistic estimates in income categories such as the following:

    a. foundation, corporate, and government grants

    b. federated campaigns (e.g., United Way, Combined Federal Campaign)

    c. special events

    d. contributions from individuals

    e. service fees

    f. publication sales

3. Make sure that the sum of the specific strategies is at least two or three times the amount that you actually need. (Not all of your efforts will be entirely successful.) For example, if you need to raise $100,000 in foundation grants, prepare proposals which, if all were funded at the amount requested, would provided you with a combined total of at least $200,000.

B.   **Establish specific strategies for each source of income.** (See sample.) Define your:

1.   goal -- include financial and other goals, such as media attention and volunteer recognition at an awards ceremony

2.   objectives -- specific, measurable results you seek to achieve to realize your overall goal

3.   primary personnel

4.   milestones -- target dates for major activities

5.   other information specific to the strategy, such as target populations, program site, collaborations with other groups, etc.

SAMPLE ANNUAL FUNDRAISING GOALS

	Last Year Actual	Best-Case Scenario	Realistic Goal
Grants			
US Dept. of Education	$ 47,500	$100,000	$ 50,000
DC Dept. of Human Services	50,000	100,000	25,000
Carnegie Corporation of New York	35,000	75,000	50,000
Ford Foundation	0	50,000	0
Meyer Foundation	10,000	25,000	10,000
Cafritz Foundation	15,000	20,000	7,500
Graham Foundation	10,000	15,000	7,500
Subtotal	**167,500**	**385,000**	**150,000**
Federated Campaigns			
United Way	12,000	30,000	15,000
Combined Federal Campaign	23,000	30,000	25,000
Subtotal	**35,000**	**60,000**	**40,000**
Special Events			
Annual Banquet	10,000	20,000	12,000
Annual Conference	5,000	10,000	4,000
Quarterly Workshops	5,000	10,000	4,000
Subtotal	**20,000**	**40,000**	**20,000**
Contributions			
Board of Directors	5,000	5,000	5,000
Spring Appeal	6,000	15,000	6,500
Summer Appeal	4,500	15,000	4,000
Fall Appeal	5,700	15,000	6,500
End-of-Year Appeal	6,800	15,000	8,000
Subtotal	**28,000**	**65,000**	**30,000**
Service Fees			
Consulting Fees	4,300	7,500	5,000
Subtotal	**4,300**	**7,500**	**5,000**
Publications Sales			
Calendar	2,800	5,000	3,000
Policy Reports	1,100	3,000	1,250
Newsletter Subscriptions	700	2,000	750
Subtotal	**4,600**	**10,000**	**5,000**
TOTAL	**$259,400**	**$567,500**	**$250,000**

SAMPLE FUNDRAISING PLAN

(Note: An organization would complete one form for each fundraising activity.)

FUNDRAISING PLAN: GRANTS

Goal: To secure $150,000 in grants, to strengthen our relationship with current grantmakers, and to initiate new relationships with additional grantmakers

Objectives:

a. To identify at least 20 good foundation, corporate, and governmental prospects

b. To prepare and submit compelling proposals to at least ten grantmakers

c. To communicate with funders on at least a quarterly basis

d. To monitor programs regularly to assure compliance with proposals

e. To keep excellent records (attendance, photographs, minutes, etc.)

f. To submit exciting progress reports and accurate financial reports on time

Primary Personnel:

a. Executive Director

b. Development Director

c. Secretary

Milestones:

January 15 - Complete research at Foundation Center and obtain guidelines

January 30 (ongoing) - Select prospects, and update this list of Milestones

January 30 (ongoing) - Add new prospects to newsletter mailing list

February 10 - Complete general support proposal

February 15 - Submit progress report to DC Dept. of Human Services

March 20 - Attend Grantmakers Conference

April 15 - Submit proposal to Cafritz Foundation

April 30 - Complete annual report for prior year

May 15 - Attend Association of Fundraising Professionals Conference

June 15 - Submit mid-year letter to update all funders, donors, and prospects

June 30 - Update list of sponsors on web page

July 15 - Submit letter of inquiry to Meyer Foundation

November 15 - Submit end-of-year letter to update all funders, donors, and prospects

---

C.	**Research grantmakers by subject, geographic location, and type of support provided.** (See "Selected Resources" at the end of this document for more details.)

1.	Visit the Foundation Center Library. It provides free use of materials on foundation and corporate giving, and the librarian can help you. Books and compact discs are also available for purchase.

2.	Visit www.technicalassistance.com. The Quick Links page provides links to a variety of foundation and governmental sites that provide information on available grants as well as other sites of interest to nonprofit organizations.

3.	Visit the website of any association of grantmakers in your region.

4.	Find out who funds organizations that are similar to yours. Look at their IRS Form 990 at Guidestar.org. Review copies of these groups' annual reports to see where they get their funding. Ask to be placed on their mailing lists.

5.	Read trade publications, such as the *Chronicle of Philanthropy*, *Foundation News and Commentary*, *Nonprofit World*, and *Nonprofit Times*. (See "Selected Resources.)

D.	**Review each grantmaker's guidelines.**

1.	If a target funder has a website, visit it, and print out all relevant information. Keep a running list or database of grant-maker names, whether the grantmaker is a good prospect, and (if so) the grantmaker deadline. (See sample.)

2.	Visit Grants.gov to sign up for automatic email alerts of new funding opportunities. Request to be put on foundations' email/mailing lists.

3.	Develop a filing system to organize grantmaker information.

SAMPLE LOG OF GRANTMAKER GUIDELINES

Foundation Name	Date Guidelines Reviewed	Good Prospect?	Deadline
Fowler Memorial Foundation	11/12	Yes	None
Meyer Foundation	11/12	No	--
Graham Fund	11/17	Yes	March 1
AT&T Foundation	12/1	No	--

E. Develop a Proposal Submission Plan. (See sample.)

1. Develop a Proposal Submission Planning Form to note priorities and procedures for each grantmaker, including:

   a. name of the grantmaker, contact person, telephone number, and mailing address

   b. which of your programs the grantmaker may support

   c. average grant size

   d. method of initial approach (e.g., letter, call, proposal)

   e. special requirements (e.g., application form, number of copies, page limitations, attachments)

   f. deadlines for inquiry letters and proposals

2. Organize your list of prospects according to their deadline dates.

3. Read each grantmaker's proposal guidelines, noting essential information on the Proposal Submission Planning Form.

4. Establish internal deadline dates for each proposal, factoring in extra time for problems and delays.

5. Add the internal and grantmaker deadline dates to your appointment calendar.

SAMPLE PROPOSAL SUBMISSION PLAN

Grantmaker Contact Information	Our Relevant Project	Average Grant Size	Preferred Method of Approach	Inquiry Letter Deadline	Special Requirements	Grant-maker Deadline	Our Internal Deadline
Community Foundation John Doe 202-123-4567	Strategic Planning	$10,000	Letter	Jan. 20	Send 3-page letter of intent focusing on organizational strengthening. Foundation may request proposal.	Jan. 20	Jan. 5
Graham Fund Jane Doe 202-123-4567	Youth Enrichment Project	$25,000	Call	N/A	Call to discuss project before submitting proposal.	Mar. 1	Feb. 15
DHHS Administration for Children & Families www.acf.hhs.gov	Youth Enrichment Project	$75,000	Proposal	N/A	Application form, attachments, and 30-page proposal required.	May 1	April 15

III. MAKE YOUR PLAN WORK

Too often, a lot of work goes into developing good plans that end up sitting on the shelf. The following tips will help you put your plan into action and stick with it over the long term:

    A.   Use your calendar.

        1.   Organize your tasks according to their ultimate deadline dates.

        2.   Establish earlier, internal deadline dates for each task, factoring in extra time for problems and delays.

        3.   Put internal and "real" deadline dates in your appointment calendar.

    B.   Get started: avoid procrastination.

        1.   Schedule an hour or two every day (or week) to develop and implement your plan. Mornings are often the best time. Treat this time just as you would an important appointment. Ask your colleagues to avoid interrupting you during this time.

        2.   Prevent the small irritations that rob you of your efficiency. Spend one session making sure that you have the supplies and documents that you need and that your materials are organized so you can find them.

        3.   At the beginning of each session (or the end of the previous session), decide what you will accomplish. Setting a reasonable goal for each session will make it easier to get started and will give you a feeling of accomplishment when you have met your goal.

        4.   Force yourself to work on your plan during the designated time. If you are having a difficult time getting started, take "baby steps" such as:

            a.   reviewing your plan

            b.   reading guidelines

      c.   proofreading the latest draft of your proposal

      d.   making sure that you have enough copies of needed documents

      e.   calling people from whom you need information or help

5.   If you are facing "writer's block," remind yourself that computers are great for editing! Type or write down your ideas however they come out. You can always rewrite and polish them later. The important thing is to get something on paper.

C. Divide up work and delegate tasks to *reliable* people.

1.   As early as possible, contact others whose help you need for items such as:

      a.   letters of support (you may have to draft these yourself)

      b.   résumés, especially from individuals who are not on staff

      c.   factual or anecdotal information

2.   Inform them of your deadline dates for their tasks.

3.   Follow up before the deadline dates to make sure work is progressing. Add follow-up dates to your calendar as soon as you delegate a task.

D. Finish up: avoid perfectionism.

1.   If you find yourself revising your plans or editing your proposal over and over again, stop and ask yourself why. Is the payoff worth the effort? If not, let it go.

2.   Remind yourself that although your organization should be presented in its best light, your work will be worthless if you miss the deadline!

IV. PREPARE A COMPELLING PROPOSAL

An effective strategy for instituting a new grantseeking campaign is to begin by developing a "generic" general support or project proposal. Depending on who your target funders are, you may want to use a common application format, such as that developed by the Washington Regional Association of Grantmakers (www.washingtongrantmakers.org). You can then revise the generic proposal to meet each grantmaker's guidelines and to emphasize each grantmaker's priorities. Here are the steps for drafting, revising, and submitting your proposal:

A. **Outline the generic proposal, including the following:**

1. Clear and Descriptive Title

2. Abstract

3. Table of Contents

4. Organizational Background

5. Need for Project (or Activities)

6. Proposed Activities

7. Expected Outcomes

8. Evaluation Plan

9. Schedule of Major Tasks

10. Staffing Pattern

11. Budget (Income and Expenses)

12. Attachments

B. Gather information

    1.   For organizational background, recycle existing documents, such as:

        a.   old proposals

        b.   recent annual reports and newsletters

        c.   information from your website

    2.   To prove there is a need for the project, gather:

        a.   facts and statistics

        b.   case studies or anecdotes from staff

        c.   information about other organizations' work (from websites, newsletters, trade publications, and networking activities)

C. Work out the details of the proposed project by contacting:

    1.   your organization's program staff

    2.   other experts in the field

    3.   prospective recipients of the service

    4.   the program officer if you have questions regarding a Request For Proposals (RFP)

D. Prepare a rough draft of the proposal by filling in the outline, writing in a clear and simple manner. Detail the following:

    1.   Organizational Background

        a.   Explain the organization's mission.

        b.   Prepare a brief history of the organization.

        c.   Summarize the organization's major accomplishments over the years.

2. Need for Project (or Activities)

   a. Explain the need, citing facts and statistics, case studies, and/or anecdotes.

   b. Describe how other organizations' similar efforts do not meet the need you seek to address.

   c. Explain why yours is the right group to address this need.

3. Proposed Project or Activities

   a. List major project activities.

   b. Describe each activity in detail.

   c. Explain why it makes sense to conduct the project in the way you've proposed. Use facts and clear arguments to back up your approach.

4. Expected Outcomes

   a. Emphasize the concrete benefits of the project to those served and to society.

   b. Brainstorm measurable results such as:

      (1) number of people to be reached

      (2) increase or decrease in a particular variable

      (3) positive actions taken by others

5. Evaluation Plan

   a. Design a plan to collect, analyze, and report data related to your expected outcomes. The plan should be appropriate to the type of project. For example, a research study requires a more complex statistical analysis than a service project.

b.   Decide which data will be collected and whether/how to collect factual information and relevant opinions from:

      (1)   clients

      (2)   staff

      (3)   other experts/professionals

      (4)   other members of the community

c.   Indicate whether staff or an outside consultant will conduct the evaluation.

d.   Explain how the evaluation results will be used and to whom they will be disseminated.

6.   Schedule of Major Tasks

a.   Briefly describe the timeline, and include a detailed chart. (See sample.)

b.   Include enough start-up time (for hiring staff, setting up the site, etc.).

c.   Assume everything will take twice as long as expected.

d.   Remember to include monitoring and evaluation activities.

SAMPLE TIMELINE 1

Project Task	Jan	Feb	Mar	Apr	May	Jun	Jul	Aug	Sep	Oct	Nov	Dec
Hire Staff	✓											
Recruit Volunteers		✓										
Train Volunteers			✓									
Hold advisory committee meetings		✓			✓			✓				
Prepare first draft of manual		✓										
Prepare second draft of manual			✓									
Finalize and print manual				✓								
Hold orientation session for clients					✓							
Hold counseling sessions for clients						✓	✓	✓	✓			
Hold wrap-up session for clients										✓		
Conduct evaluation meetings				✓		✓			✓		✓	
Submit reports to grantmaker						✓						✓

SAMPLE TIMELINE 2

Target Dates	Activity	Purpose/Outcome	Personnel
January 31	Hire staff. Recruit and train volunteers.	All project personnel are prepare to begin working by January 31.	Project Director
February, May, and August	Conduct Advisory Committee meetings.	Experts will discuss project plans and activities to assess progress and to provide guidance.	Executive Director
April 30	Complete and print manual.	Clients will have comprehensive, written instructions on how to do project activity.	Project Director
May 1 through October 31	Conduct weekly sessions with clients (orientation, counseling, and wrap-up).	Clients will be provided with guidance and information on how to implement project activity.	Project Director, Counselor, Volunteers
April, June, September, and November	Conduct evaluation meetings.	Project staff and evaluator will discuss evaluation plan, data collection, and data analysis to assess progress and address any challenges that may arise.	Executive Director, Project Director, Evaluation Consultant
December 31	Complete project report and submit to funder and other service providers.	Funder will receive an analysis of project successes and challenges. Lessons learned will be shared with other groups. Project activities can be replicated by other groups.	Project Director

7. Staffing Pattern

    a. Break out tasks into short job descriptions.

        (1) Describe the role of paid staff, including responsibilities, to whom they will report, whom they will supervise, and the percentage of their time they will spend working on the project. Remember to include a portion of administrative staff's salaries (accountant, receptionist, etc.).

        (2) Describe the role of advisory committee members and/or consultants. Advisory committees and consultants can be utilized to fill gaps in staff expertise.

    b. Include brief biographies describing the qualifications of staff, consultants, key volunteers, and advisors. Attach résumés.

    c. Describe the role of volunteers, necessary qualifications, and how they will be recruited, trained, and supervised.

    d. Present an organizational chart for your entire staff as well as for the project staff. (See sample.)

SAMPLE PROJECT ORGANIZATIONAL CHART

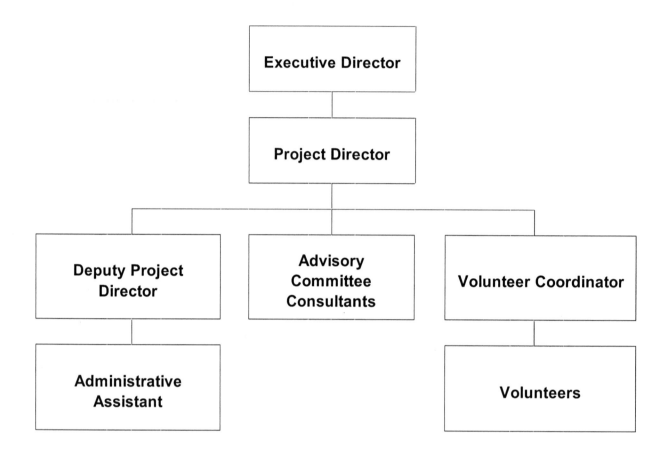

8. Budget (See sample.)

    a. List projected expenses.

        (1) Salaries

        (2) Program Expenses

        (3) Administrative (Overhead or Office) Expenses

    b. List projected income, indicating whether each line item has been received or is anticipated.

    c. Make sure all dollar amounts are real and reasonable figures. Get price quotes from vendors, and find out salaries of individuals in comparable positions.

    d. Include budget notes where appropriate to explain how you arrived at your figures and/or what materials or services the figure encompasses.

    e. Always include at least a portion of overhead expenses and administrative personnel in project budgets.

    f. Administrative and fundraising expenses combined should comprise less than 35% of the total budget.

    g. Some funders will want to know your long-term fundraising plans to maintain the program. Include a brief narrative and your Fundraising Goals chart.

9. Clear and Descriptive Title

    a. Create a short, descriptive title that is not cumbersome.

10. Table of Contents and Abstract

    a. If the proposal is more than ten pages, include a Table of Contents and a one- to two-page Abstract in front.

    b. Remember to update the Table of Contents each time you edit the proposal.

SAMPLE PROJECT BUDGET

Salaries & Benefits	Year One	Year Two[1]
Executive Director (20% of $120,000)	$ 24,000	$ 25,200
Program Director (100% of $90,000)	$ 90,000	$ 94,500
Deputy Program Director (100% of $70,000)	$ 70,000	$ 73,500
Volunteer Coordinator (100% of $64,000)	$ 64,000	$ 67,200
Accountant (10% of $70,000)	$ 7,000	$ 7,350
Administrative Assistant (50% of $48,000)	$ 24,000	$ 25,200
Benefits (20% of salaries)	$ 55,800	$ 58,590
Subtotals	**$ 334,800**	**$ 351,540**
Program Expenses		
Advisory Committee Honorariums[2]	$ 7,500	$ 0
Printing of Manual[3]	$ 750	$ 788
Production of Public Service Announcement	$ 2,000	$ 0
Six Counseling Sessions[4]	$ 3,000	$ 3,150
Miscellaneous	$ 500	$ 525
Subtotal	**$ 13,750**	**$ 4,463**
Administrative Expenses		
Rental of Office & Utilities	$ 12,000	$ 12,600
Telephones	$ 2,400	$ 2,520
Delivery/Postage	$ 1,800	$ 1,890
Supplies	$ 3,600	$ 3,780
Photocopying	$ 1,200	$ 1,260
Subtotal	**$ 21,000**	**$ 22,050**
TOTAL EXPENSES	**$ 369,550**	**$ 378,053**
Secured Income		
Carnegie Corporation of New York	$ 150,000	$ 150,000
Ford Foundation	$ 100,000	$ 100,000
Cafritz Foundation	$ 50,000	$ 0
Subtotal	**$ 300,000**	**$ 250,000**
Anticipated Income		
Meyer Foundation	$ 25,000	$ 0
Rockefeller Foundation	$ 25,000	$ 0
Combined Federal Campaign	$ 10,000	$ 10,000
Program Registration Fees	$ 10,000	$ 10,000
Subtotal	**$ 70,000**	**$ 20,000**
TOTAL INCOME	**$ 370,000**	**$ 270,000**

[1]A five percent increase to cover inflation has been calculated for expense items in Year Two
[2]Ten members, three meetings, $250 honorarium per meeting per member
[3]500 copies printed @ $1.50 each
[4]Space rental @ $200 per session, refreshments @ $300 per session

Technical Assistance & Support Consultants

E. Edit the proposal

1. The key to good writing is rewriting. Expect to revise your proposal several times before and after you share it with your colleagues.

2. At the beginning of each section, include an overview paragraph to help orient the reader. The rest of the section should expand upon the ideas introduced in the overview paragraph. Conclude the section with a summary statement, predictions, or a plan of action.

3. Within each section, make logical connections among the various facts and ideas. The following are some ways in which you can organize your ideas:

   a. Problem → causes → effects → solutions

   b. Possible actions → advantages → disadvantages → selected course of action

   c. Chronological order of events or actions to be taken

   d. Order of importance of events or ideas

   e. Order of interest (e.g., beginning with an attention-grabbing fact)

   f. Alphabetical or numerical order

4. Use the following three types of writing appropriately to describe, analyze, and reflect upon your issue/work:

   a. Description -- an explanation of key features, clearly and logically ordered and sufficiently detailed such that the reader can understand and visualize what is being described.

   b. Analysis -- an interpretation of reasons, motives, and significance, based on facts that have been described, such that the reader can understand the thought processes behind the conclusions that have been reached.

c. Reflection -- a type of analysis that also incorporates a judgement, based on facts and reasoning, regarding what should be done differently, the same way, or not at all.

5. Adopt the habits of good writers:

   a. Use the active voice.

   b. Be brief.

   c. Be clear.

   d. Be positive and specific.

6. Kick the habits of bad writers:

   a. Hedging -- being vague or indirect

   b. Using too many words

   c. Using big words, jargon, or acronyms

   d. Faking sincerity

7. Make use of these additional writing tips:

   a. Vary sentence length and structure.

   b. Avoid using the same word repeatedly.

   c. Select a tone of voice appropriate to the nature of the topic (e.g., serious or lighthearted).

   d. Consider whether the particular section should be informative, pleasantly persuasive, or entertaining -- and choose your words accordingly.

   e. Imagine the type of people likely to read the proposal, and write directly to them. What do they need to know? What is important and interesting to them?

f.   Write with authority.

g.   Be very careful about using humor, sarcasm, and anger. These can backfire.

F.   Format the proposal.

1.   Use one readable font -- nothing too exotic or too small.

2.   Use visual devices to enhance your document, but exercise restraint. If you overuse them, the reader will be distracted and annoyed instead of impressed with your creativity. The following are commonly used visual devices:

a.   Headings and subheadings

b.   Bold, italics, underlining, and screens/shading

c.   Page and paragraph numbers

d.   Bullets and lists

e.   Indentations

f.   Headers and footers

g.   Pull-quotes

h.   Varying font style, size, and color

i.   Charts, graphs, illustrations, and photos

j.   Captions

k.   Boxes, borders, and rules/lines

G.   Evaluate the "big picture."

1.   Is what you are proposing to do clear? Will it address the problem/issue?

2. Is the proposal written in a manner appropriate for the target funders? Does it address their concerns?

3. Is it interesting, persuasive, and informative? Does it present something new?

4. Is the content presented in an organized and logical manner?

5. Does one section flow into the next?

6. Is there balance among sections?

7. Have all essential issues or points been included?

8. Does it provide the "right" amount of detail?

9. Does it get to the point?

10. Is the overall format appropriate, appealing, and easy to read?

H. Evaluate the "little picture."

1. Grammar

   a. Do the subject and verb agree?

   b. Is the correct tense being used?

   c. Has an adjective been used instead of an adverb (or vice versa)?

   d. Has the correct pronoun been used?

2. Punctuation

   a. Are commas used correctly?

   b. Are quotation marks used correctly, especially with periods and commas?

      c.   Are apostrophes used correctly to show possession or contractions?

      d.   Are hyphens used correctly to form a compound adjective?

3.   Spelling and Capitalization

      a.   Has a computerized spell check been conducted?

      b.   Have all names and foreign words been checked?

      c.   Have words been capitalized correctly, especially in titles?

4.   Facts and Figures

      a.   Have facts been checked and documented?

      b.   Have all numbers been checked?

      c.   Are calculations correct?

5.   Visual Organization

      a.   Is the font reader-friendly?

      b.   Have visual organization techniques been used judiciously?

I.   Prepare the inquiry letters.

1.   If any of your target funders require a letter of inquiry, write a short letter summarizing the main points of the proposal and requesting permission to submit a full proposal. (Adhere to the grantmakers' page-length requirements.)

J.   Tailor the generic proposal for each grantmaker.

1.   Follow the funder's instructions! Reread each grantmaker's guidelines, and revise the "generic" proposal as necessary to make sure that your proposal meets all requirements.

2.   Gather attachments requested by the grantmaker.

3. Have someone with a "fresh eye" and excellent writing skills proofread the proposal. Be sure to give the proofreader the guidelines so that they can check to see if you missed anything.

K. Prepare the cover letter.

1. Write a short cover letter summarizing the project, how the project fits into the funder's interest areas, and the amount requested.

2. Direct the program officer to a contact person on staff who is knowledgeable about the proposal and will be accessible.

3. Have the organization's highest official sign the cover letter.

L. Submit the proposal.

1. Photocopy the required number of copies. Remember to keep a copy of the complete application package for your files.

2. Staple or clip the proposal together. If the grantmaker says, "no binder," do not use a binder.

3. Use the mail, an overnight delivery service, or a messenger based on how much time remains before the deadline. (Remember that some funders may think that you are wasteful if you use overnight delivery services.)

4. If there is any question in your mind about whether the proposal was received, follow up with a telephone call.

SAMPLE INSTRUCTIONS: The Project Description

Department of Health and Human Services
Agency for Children and Families
American Recovery and Reinvestment Act of 2009
Strengthening Communities Fund-Nonprofit Capacity Building Program

The project description provides the majority of information by which an application is evaluated and ranked in competition with other applications for available assistance. The project description should be concise and complete. It should address the activity for which Federal funds are being requested. Supporting documents should be included where they can present information clearly and succinctly. In preparing the project description, information that is responsive to each of the requested evaluation criteria must be provided. Awarding offices use this and other information in making their funding recommendations. It is important, therefore, that this information be included in the application in a manner that is clear and complete.

ACF is particularly interested in specific project descriptions that focus on outcomes and convey strategies for achieving intended performance. Project descriptions are evaluated on the basis of substance and measurable outcomes, not length. Extensive exhibits are not required. Cross-referencing should be used rather than repetition. Supporting information concerning activities that will not be directly funded by the grant or information that does not directly pertain to an integral part of the grant-funded activity should be placed in an appendix.

Applicants that are required to submit a full project description shall prepare the project description statement in accordance with the following instructions while being aware of the specified evaluation criteria. The text options give a broad overview of what the project description should include while the evaluation criteria identify the measures that will be used to evaluate applications.

Table of Contents
List the contents of the application including corresponding page numbers.

Project Summary/Abstract
Provide a summary of the project description (one page or less) with reference to the funding request.

Objectives and Need for Assistance

Clearly identify the physical, economic, social, financial, institutional, and/or other problem(s) requiring a solution. The need for assistance must be demonstrated and the principal and subordinate objectives of the project must be clearly stated; supporting documentation, such as letters of support and testimonials from concerned interests other than the applicant, may be included. Any relevant data based on planning studies should be included or referred to in the endnotes/footnotes. Incorporate demographic data and participant/ beneficiary information, as needed. In developing the project description, the applicant may volunteer or be requested to provide information on the total range of projects currently being conducted and supported (or to be initiated), some of which may be outside the scope of the program announcement.

Results or Benefits Expected

Identify the results and benefits to be derived.

Approach

Outline a plan of action that describes the scope and detail of how the proposed work will be accomplished. Account for all functions or activities identified in the application. Cite factors that might accelerate or decelerate the work and state your reason for taking the proposed approach rather than others. Describe any unusual features of the project such as design or technological innovations, reductions in cost or time, or extraordinary social and community involvement.

Provide quantitative monthly or quarterly projections of the accomplishments to be achieved for each function or activity in such terms as the number of people to be served and the number of activities accomplished.

When accomplishments cannot be quantified by activity or function, list them in chronological order to show the schedule of accomplishments and their target dates.

If any data is to be collected, maintained, and/or disseminated, clearance may be required from OMB. This clearance pertains to any "collection of information that is conducted or sponsored by ACF."

Provide a list of organizations, cooperating entities, consultants, or other key individuals who will work on the project along with a short description of the nature of their effort or contribution.

Evaluation

Provide a narrative addressing how the conduct of the project and the results of the project will be evaluated. In addressing the evaluation of results, state how you will determine the extent to which the project has achieved its stated objectives and the extent to which the accomplishment of objectives can be attributed to the project. Discuss the criteria to be used to evaluate results, and explain the methodology that will be used to determine if the needs identified and discussed are being met and if the project results and benefits are being achieved. With respect to the conduct of the project, define the procedures to be employed to determine whether the project is being conducted in a manner consistent with the work plan presented and discuss the impact of the project's various activities that address the project's effectiveness.

Geographic Location

Describe the precise location of the project and boundaries of the area to be served by the proposed project. Maps or other graphic aids may be attached.

Additional Information

The following are requests for additional information that must be included in the application:

Eligibility Certification

Applicants must provide the following as certification of their eligibility under this program announcement. Please provide: Proof of Non-Profit Status. Non-profit organizations applying for funding are required to submit proof of their non-profit status. Proof of non-profit status is any one of the following:

- A reference to the applicant organization's listing in the IRS's most recent list of tax-exempt organizations described in the IRS Code.

- A copy of a currently valid IRS tax-exemption certificate.

- A statement from a State taxing body, State attorney general, or other appropriate State official certifying that the applicant organization has non-profit status and that none of the net earnings accrue to any private shareholders or individuals.

- A certified copy of the organization's certificate of incorporation or similar document that clearly establishes non-profit status.

- Any of the items in the subparagraphs immediately above for a State or national parent organization and a statement signed by the parent organization that the applicant organization is a local non-profit affiliate.

When applying electronically, proof of non-profit status may be submitted as an attachment; however, proof of non-profit status must be submitted prior to award.

Logic Model
Applicants are expected to use a model for designing and managing their project. A logic model is a tool that presents the conceptual framework for a proposed project and explains the linkages among program elements. While there are many versions of the logic model, they generally summarize the logical connections among the needs that are the focus of the project, project goals and objectives, the target population, project inputs (resources), the proposed activities/processes/outputs directed toward the target population, the expected short- and long-term outcomes the initiative is designed to achieve, and the evaluation plan for measuring the extent to which proposed processes and outcomes actually occur.

Staff and Position Data
Provide a biographical sketch and job description for each key person appointed. Job descriptions for each vacant key position should be included as well. As new key staff is appointed, biographical sketches will also be required.

Organizational Profiles
Provide information on the applicant organization(s) and cooperating partners, such as: organizational charts; financial statements; audit reports or statements from Certified Public Accountants/Licensed Public Accountants; Employer Identification Number(s); contact persons and telephone numbers; names of bond carriers; child care licenses and other documentation of professional accreditation; information on compliance with Federal/State/local government standards; documentation of experience in the program area; and, other pertinent information.

Third-Party Agreements
Provide written and signed agreements between grantees and subgrantees, or subcontractors, or other cooperating entities. These agreements must detail the scope of work to be performed, work

schedules, remuneration, and other terms and conditions that structure or define the relationship.

Letters of Support
Provide statements from community, public, and commercial leaders that support the project proposed for funding. All submissions should be included in the application package or by the application deadline.

Budget and Budget Justification
Provide a budget with line-item detail and detailed calculations for each budget object class identified on the Budget Information Form (SF-424A or SF-424C). Detailed calculations must include estimation methods, quantities, unit costs, and other similar quantitative detail sufficient for the calculation to be duplicated. If matching is a requirement, include a breakout by the funding sources identified in Block 15 of the SF-424.

Provide a narrative budget justification that describes how the categorical costs are derived. Discuss the necessity, reasonableness, and allocation of the proposed costs.

V. BUILD LONG-TERM RELATIONSHIPS WITH FUNDERS

The old adage in business is, "It's easier to keep a customer than to get a new one." The same is true of funders. Here are some steps you should take to stay in your funders' good graces:

A. Complete tasks as promised.

1. If your organization has separate development and program staffs, make sure that the program staff has -- and periodically reviews -- a copy of the proposal.

2. Make sure that the program staff understands the relationship between completing the project or activity as proposed and being able to obtain future funding from existing supporters as well as future supporters. (People, especially grantmakers, are likely to talk to each other about your organization.)

3. Check with program staff periodically to make sure work is progressing on schedule. Add the major tasks from your timeline to your appointment book or calendar as a reminder.

B. Keep good records.

1. Collect data on relevant characteristics of your target population before and after the project so you will be able to measure changes.

2. Take attendance at meetings and events.

3. Record, videotape, and/or photograph activities.

4. Have participants fill out evaluation forms.

5. Keep a journal to note problems and opportunities as they arise, as well as to keep a record of interesting anecdotes.

6. Get receipts for all expenses.

7. Note all volunteer hours contributed.

8. Keep track of donated materials and services.

C. Write detailed and compelling progress reports, annual reports, and newsletter articles touting your work.

1. Use the format of the proposal as a guide for preparing your report if the grantmaker does not provide a specific reporting format. Submit the reports on time.

2. Include factual data (numbers of people served, etc.).

3. Include opinions of clients, experts, and community members.

4. Include personal anecdotes to make your work come alive.

5. Describe outcomes in the best light possible.

   a. For objectives that were not fully achieved:

      (1) Explain why and take responsibility -- don't try to blame it on some other organization or person. Think about what your organization should have done to ensure success.

      (2) Explain what was done instead to ensure that the project would still proceed. Be creative here.

      (3) Explain how the overall goal was still achieved.

   b. For objectives that were achieved:

      (1) Describe accomplishments with enthusiasm and in detail. Include lists, samples, copies of products, copies of print publicity received, photographs, etc.

      (2) Focus on the benefits to your target population as well as the broader community or society.

      (3) Include client testimonials as well as endorsements from outsiders.

D. Engage in ongoing communication with the program officer and other supporters.

1. Remember to thank all funders, volunteers, and supporters.

2. Call the program officer, major donor, or corporate sponsor to communicate major problems or opportunities.

3. Make sure that you are well-prepared for meetings and/or site visits with grantmakers, sponsors, and donors.

4. Put grantmakers, donors, and volunteers on your mailing list to receive copies of your organization's print and/or electronic newsletter and other publications.

5. Send grantmakers, donors, and volunteers invitations to your events.

6. Send grantmakers, donors, and volunteers holiday greetings.

7. Send grantmakers and major donors copies of articles about your issue or organization that may be of interest to them.

VI. FACTORS AFFECTING THE GIVING DECISION

Use this checklist to evaluate your organization's fundraising efforts. Each "no" answer indicates an area you need to improve.

A. Your Organization's Qualifications

1. Is your organization incorporated?

2. Has it obtained its 501(c)(3) status?

3. Does it adhere to generally accepted accounting procedures?

4. Does it have the human resources necessary to carry out the proposed activities?

5. Do proposed personnel have the necessary skills, training, experience, and contacts?

6. Does your organization have access to needed material resources such as meeting space or equipment? If not, does it have a solid plan to get these resources?

7. Does your organization have a viable plan to underwrite the project over the long term?

B. Your Organization's Presentation

1. Have you documented the need for the project?

2. Is your analysis and presentation of the problem compelling?

3. Does your presentation show that you are aware of other relevant initiatives?

4. Does your organization collaborate with other groups doing related work?

5. Is your plan to address the need likely to succeed?

6. Is the timetable realistic?

7. Is the project innovative and unique in some way rather than duplicating other efforts?

8. Are costs reasonable when compared to expected outcomes (such as the number of individuals served)?

9. Have you shown that your organization has the capacity to carry out the activities successfully?

10. Have you indicated measurable results and outcomes?

11. Have you described a plan to monitor and evaluate progress?

12. Is the proposal, solicitation letter, or invitation well-written, free from errors, and attractively (but inexpensively) presented?

C. Appropriate Selection of Fundraising Strategy

1. Has your organization analyzed its strengths and weaknesses as they pertain to fundraising?

2. Has your organization carefully analyzed several fundraising strategies to determine what resources are required for success?

3. Has you organization selected fundraising strategies that rely primarily on resources that your organization already possesses or can obtain?

D. Appropriate Selection of Funder

1. Does your organization and/or project address an issue of concern to the funder?

2. Is your organization within the funder's target locale?

3. Are you requesting a type of support that the funder provides? For example, some grantmakers will not give general support.

E. Adherence to Guidelines

1. Have you followed the funder's guidelines? Did you provide all requested information and documentation?

2. Is your request for funds within the funder's range? Asking for too much or too little can be a problem.

3. Have the proper people signed or endorsed the proposal or solicitation?

4. Did you submit the proposal before the deadline?

F. Your Organization's Track Record

1. Does your organization have a history of providing high-quality, cost-effective services?

2. Has your organization diligently fulfilled its prior commitments to funders, both in terms of program implementation and reporting requirements?

3. Has you organization given credit to its supporters in its written materials and at organizational events?

SELECTED RESOURCES

Grants.gov
www.grants.gov

Grants.gov allows organizations to electronically find and apply for competitive grant opportunities from all federal grantmaking agencies. Individuals may sign up to receive free funding alerts by email.

Foundation Center Library
www.fdncenter.org

The Foundation Center provides free use of materials on foundation and corporate giving as well as nonprofit management. Books and compact discs are also available for purchase.

Technical Assistance & Support Consultants
P.O. Box 69
Mount Rainier, MD 20712-0069
www.technicalassistance.com

TASC is a consulting firm that assists progressive organizations with fund development, writing and publishing, and grantsmanship training. The website provides links to information on available grants as well as other sites of interest to nonprofit organizations.

Organizations Similar to Yours

Visit their websites, look at their profiles on Guidestar.org, and request copies of their annual reports to see where they get their funding. Ask to be placed on their mailing lists.

W.K. Kellogg Foundation Logic Model Development Guide
http://www.wkkf.org/Pubs/Tools/Evaluation/Pub3669.pdf

Funders are increasingly requiring logic models to be included with proposal submissions. This free guide focuses on the development and use of the program logic model.

Chronicle of Philanthropy

www.philanthropy.com

This is a biweekly newspaper specifically focused on fundraising.

Nonprofit World

www.snpo.org

The Society for Nonprofit Organizations publishes this bimonthly magazine and monthly, on-line funding alerts.

The Nonprofit Times

www.nptimes.com

This magazine focuses on issues related to nonprofit organizations and is published 18 times per year.

Board Source

www.boardsource.org

This organization provides resources and leadership tools to help build stronger nonprofit boards and organizations.

Idealist and Action Without Borders

www.nonprofits.org

This website provides a wealth of information as well as links to dozens of other sites of interest to nonprofit organizations.

GLOSSARY OF TERMS

Abstract

A brief summary of the purpose, importance, and scope of a proposed project or program

Budget

A list of estimated income and expenses, by category and amount, for a particular project or program during a defined period

Budget Narrative

A narrative explanation of what is included in each budget item and how the amount was calculated or determined

Catalog of Federal Domestic Assistance (CFDA)

An online database of all federal programs available to state and local governments; federally-recognized Indian tribal governments; territories and possessions of the United States; domestic public, quasi-public, and private profit and nonprofit organizations and institutions; specialized groups; and individuals

CFDA Number

The identifying number that a federal program is assigned in the Catalog of Federal Domestic Assistance (CFDA)

Continuation Grant

A grant that provides additional funding for budget periods subsequent to the initial budget period

Cooperative Agreement

An award of financial assistance that provides for substantial involvement between the awarding agency and the recipient during the performance of the contemplated activity

Discretionary Grant   A grant (or cooperative agreement) for which the awarding agency: may select the recipient(s) from among all eligible recipients; may decide to make or not make an award based on the programmatic, technical, or scientific content of an application; and may decide the amount of funding to be awarded (as opposed to "formula grant")

DUNS Number   A nine-digit identification number provided by the commercial company Dun & Bradstreet (D&B) through its Data Universal Numbering System

Equipment   Tangible nonexpendable personal property charged to the grant award and having a useful life of more than one year and, usually, an acquisition cost of $5,000 or more per unit

Evaluation   A process to determine the significance or effectiveness of a project, program, or activity by careful appraisal and study

Formula Grant   A grant that a federal agency is directed by Congress to make to grantees, for which the amount is established by a formula based on certain criteria that are written into the legislation and program regulations (as opposed to "discretionary grant")

Funder   The agency, foundation, corporation, or organization offering a grant (also called the "grantor")

Funding Opportunity Notice   A publicly available document by which a federal agency makes known its intentions to award discretionary grants or cooperative agreements, usually as a result of a competition for funds (also known as a program announcement, notice of funding availability, solicitation, request for proposals, request for applications, etc.)

Funding Opportunity Number	The number that a federal agency assigns to its grant announcement (generally available on the funding opportunity notice and at www.grants.gov)
Funding Period	The period of time when federal funding is available for obligation by the recipient
Grant	An award of financial assistance that provides support to accomplish a public purpose
Grant Agreement	A legal instrument for the transfer of funds from the funder to the grantee and which sets forth the terms and conditions of the award
Grant Award Notification	An official document containing the amount, terms, and conditions of an award for a discretionary grant or cooperative agreement that is signed by a program official who is authorized to obligate the agency in financial matters
Grant Seeker	The organization or individual applying for a grant
Grantee	The recipient of a grant award
Grantor	The agency, foundation, corporation, or organization offering a grant (also called the "funder")
Indirect Costs	Facilities and administrative costs incurred for common or joint purposes that therefore cannot be identified readily and specifically with a particular project or program (as opposed to direct costs)

Matching Funds	Funds required to pay the percentage of project costs not covered by a grant and therefore contributed by the grant recipient
Outcomes	Results of the program, services, or products provided, such as changes in knowledge, attitude, or behavior that are expected to occur as a result of implementing the project, program, service, or activity
Outputs	The direct products of program activities, which and may include types, levels, and targets of services to be delivered by the program (e.g., ten full-day professional development workshops attended by a total of 300 elementary school teachers)
Partnership	Organizations helping each other to meet their respective, complementary goals
Program Income	Gross income earned by the award recipient that is directly generated or earned as a result of the award
Project Costs	All allowable costs incurred by an award recipient and the value of the contributions made by third parties in accomplishing the objectives of the award during the project period
Project Period	The period of time established in the award document during which the awarding agency sponsorship begins and ends
Proposal	A document submitted to a grantor describing a project, program, service, or activity and the associated budget for which grant funds or a cooperative agreement is sought

Request for Applications (RFA)	The document that describes the requirements for a grant application or proposal
Request for Proposals (RFP)	The document that describes the requirements for a grant application or proposal
Reviewer	A qualified individual who serves on a panel or team responsible for reviewing, scoring, and recommending applicants for grant awards
State Single Point of Contact (SPOC)	An agency or office designated by a state under Executive Order 12372, "Intergovernmental Review of Federal Programs," to learn about and comment on selected projects affecting the jurisdiction
Supplies	All personal property used in the performance of work under a funding agreement (excluding equipment, intangible property, debt instruments, and inventions of a contractor)
Vetting	A process through with an individual or organization is evaluated for possible approval or acceptance

ABOUT TASC

Technical Assistance & Support Consultants (TASC) assists progressive organizations with institutional development. Established in 1991, TASC has specialized expertise, broad experience, and a track record of success in the areas of: grant research, proposal development, report writing, training/ coaching, publishing, and other management support services.

TASC is committed to advancing progressive causes by providing our clients with cost-effective services of exceptional quality. TASC can serve as a creative source of new ideas as well as tried-and-true methods. TASC is action oriented and focuses on obtaining results. Our clients depend on us to get the job done right and on time.

What are the benefits of using TASC?

Many large organizations regularly utilize outside specialists to help them avoid or solve problems. Smaller organizations -- which are less likely to have the manpower to devote to tasks that are labor intensive or require specialized skills -- can also reap great benefits from the use of consultants.

TASC can provide your organization with a fresh perspective on its development program based on almost three decades of experience with nonprofits addressing such issues as child development, health, education, poverty, housing and homelessness, community development, and foreign policy toward Africa and the Caribbean.

Our clients have discovered that:

*   TASC helps nonprofits respond quickly to emerging needs without neglecting ongoing programs.

*   TASC can be more cost-effective than hiring full-time staff or reassigning current personnel.

*   TASC provides flexibility because there need not be a long-term obligation.

*   TASC expands and enhances staff capabilities to help organizations realize their goals.

**For more information,
please visit www.technicalassistance.com**

CPSIA information can be obtained at www.ICGtesting.com
Printed in the USA
LVOW021734111011

250060LV00004B/10/P